AF431214

Zodiacal Herbage

Zodiacal Herbage

Astrological Insights: volume 1

Matthew Petchinsky

Apophis Enterprises LLC

Copyright © 2024 by Matthew Petchinsky

All rights reserved. No part of this book may be reproduced in any manner whatsoever without written permission except in the case of brief quotations embodied in critical articles and reviews.

First Printing, 2024

Zodiacal Herbage: Astrological Insights: Volume 1
By: Matthew Petchinsky

Introduction: Bridging the Zodiac with Botanicals
Overview

In the intricate web of existence, ancient wisdom has often provided pathways to understanding the deeper connections between nature and human life. In this volume, *Zodiacal Herbage: Astrological Insights*, we delve into the fascinating concept of linking zodiac signs and their corresponding energies with specific herbs. This approach aims to empower readers in enhancing their personal health and spiritual growth by integrating two age-old practices: astrology and herbalism. These disciplines, steeped in centuries of tradition, share a common belief in the interconnectedness of the universe, where celestial bodies and earthly flora harmonize to influence our lives.

Purpose

The purpose of this book is to offer readers a comprehensive guide to harnessing the profound powers of both astrology and herbalism. By understanding how astrological energies align with specific botanicals, we can tailor our herbal use to align with our own unique astrological makeup. Whether you are seeking balance, vitality, or spiritual elevation, this book provides practical tools and insights to navigate your journey. Our aim is to demystify these ancient arts and help readers use them to foster personal empowerment, health, and spiritual well-being.

Methodology

In approaching this work, we have meticulously paired each zodiac sign with herbs that resonate with its unique attributes and energies. The methodology relies on both historical texts and modern astrological understanding to identify herbs that are in tune with each sign's ruling planets, elemental association, and characteristic energies. For example, Aries, ruled by Mars and associated with fire, will be matched with herbs known for their stimulating and energizing properties. Each chapter will explore a zodiac sign's strengths, challenges, and specific traits, followed by detailed descriptions of herbs that best align with these attributes. Furthermore, each herbal pairing will include practical recommendations for use, offering readers guidance on how to incorporate these botanicals into their daily lives, whether through teas, tinctures, essential oils, or rituals.

In this book, you will discover a fresh perspective on the cosmos and nature's bounty, woven together to enrich your journey toward a balanced and harmonious life. Whether you are new to astrology or a seasoned herbalist, *Zodiacal Herbage* invites you to explore this ancient fusion of knowledge and find deeper connections within yourself and the world around you.

Check out my Virtual dispensary for all your hemp needs: https://shift.store/sg1fan23477/retail

Chapter 1: Aries and Its Energetic Herbs

Aries Traits

The astrological sign of Aries, the first of the zodiac, is ruled by Mars and embodies fiery, pioneering qualities. Those born under Aries are often recognized for their boundless energy, courage, and determination. They exude a spirit of adventure, facing challenges head-on with an innate desire to lead and explore new territories. This cardinal fire sign is known for its dynamic nature, seeking novelty and action at every turn. Aries individuals are characterized by their ambition, fearlessness, and ability to motivate others, making them natural leaders. However, their drive can sometimes lead to impatience, impulsiveness, and a tendency to rush into situations without considering potential consequences. Their fiery spirit demands outlets to express creativity and conquer challenges, making it essential for Aries to maintain a balance that allows them to channel their energy positively.

Herbal Alignments

Given the energetic and ambitious nature of Aries, it's essential to find herbs that complement and support their drive. The following herbs have been selected to enhance their natural qualities while providing soothing and balancing effects.

1. **Nettle (Urtica dioica)**

   Nettle is an excellent ally for Aries due to its invigorating and strengthening properties. It is rich in vitamins and minerals, particularly iron, which is crucial for maintaining high energy levels. Aries individuals can be prone to burnouts because of their relentless pace, and nettle can help replenish their energy reserves and fortify their bodies. Nettle tea or infusions offer a gentle, sustained boost of vitality, aiding in detoxification and promoting healthy circulation.

   Recipe - Nettle Infusion:
   - 1 cup dried nettle leaves

- 1 quart boiling water

Place the dried nettle leaves in a quart jar, cover with boiling water, and let steep for 4-8 hours. Strain and drink the infusion over the next 24 hours. This simple yet powerful infusion can be sipped throughout the day to maintain energy and clarity.

2. **Basil (Ocimum basilicum)**

Basil is another herb that aligns well with Aries' characteristics. As a warming herb, it complements Aries' fiery temperament and enhances their focus and mental clarity. Its uplifting aroma can also help lift their spirits, which can sometimes be dampened by frustrations arising from impatience. Basil has been traditionally used to reduce stress, alleviate fatigue, and promote clarity of mind.

Recipe - Basil Oil:

- 1 cup fresh basil leaves
- 1 cup olive oil

Wash and dry the basil leaves thoroughly. In a small saucepan, gently heat the olive oil until warm but not boiling. Add the basil leaves and allow them to infuse over low heat for 10 minutes. Let the oil cool, then strain and store in a glass bottle. Use this fragrant oil in cooking or massage it onto sore muscles to soothe and invigorate.

Conclusion

For Aries individuals, herbal alignments such as nettle and basil can be powerful allies in nurturing their dynamic and pioneering spirit. Nettle infusions can sustain their energy levels, while basil oil and teas can help sharpen focus and alleviate stress. By understanding and using these herbs, Aries can harness their innate drive to lead, create, and explore, all while maintaining a balanced state that supports their fiery nature. As we journey further into the zodiac, we will continue to explore more herbal alignments for each sign, offering insights and recipes to enhance personal growth and spiritual alignment.

Check out my Virtual dispensary for all your hemp needs: https://shift.store/sg1fan23477/retail

Chapter 2: Taurus and Its Grounding Herbs

Taurus Characteristics

Taurus, the second sign of the zodiac, is ruled by Venus and embodies the qualities of earthiness, stability, and sensuality. As a fixed earth sign, Taurus is known for its steadfastness, practicality, and appreciation for the tangible pleasures in life. Those born under this sign exhibit loyalty, patience, and an unwavering dedication to their goals. They take pride in creating a comfortable, beautiful environment around them, often gravitating towards aesthetics, nature, and sensory experiences. Taurus individuals thrive in routine and seek security, preferring to build a solid foundation before pursuing new ventures.

Their determination and persistence allow them to excel in long-term projects, but their affinity for routine can make them resistant to change. Additionally, the inherent love for comfort and luxury may sometimes lead to indulgence and stubbornness. Taurus benefits from practices that help maintain their grounding energy while also encouraging adaptability and preventing stagnation.

Herbal Alignments

Taurus aligns well with herbs that provide stability and comfort, helping them stay grounded while also supporting flexibility and balance. Thyme and spearmint are two herbs that align with the earthy nature of Taurus.

1. **Thyme (Thymus vulgaris)**

   Thyme is a warming and aromatic herb that supports Taurus by promoting strength, protection, and overall well-being. It has antimicrobial and antioxidant properties, making it ideal for cleansing the body and mind. Taurus often seeks comfort and familiarity, and thyme provides both with its soothing aroma and ability to bolster the immune system. Furthermore, its grounding energy can help Taurus maintain stability and focus, especially during stressful times.

Recipe - Thyme Foot Soak:
- ½ cup dried thyme leaves
- 4 cups boiling water
- 2 tablespoons sea salt

  Pour boiling water over the dried thyme leaves and allow them to steep for 20 minutes. Strain and mix the thyme infusion with the sea salt. Pour the mixture into a basin or tub and add enough warm water to soak your feet comfortably. Relax and soak for 20-30 minutes. This foot soak is excellent for relaxation, easing tension, and reinvigorating the senses.

2. **Spearmint (Mentha spicata)**

Spearmint, a cooling herb with a refreshing aroma, helps Taurus balance their desire for stability with adaptability. It promotes mental clarity and alleviates mental fatigue, providing Taurus with a clear head to make rational decisions without being overwhelmed by stubbornness or indecision. Spearmint is also soothing to the digestive system, often providing relief from indulgence-related discomfort.

Recipe - Spearmint Tea:
- 1 tablespoon dried spearmint leaves
- 1 cup boiling water

Pour boiling water over the dried spearmint leaves and let them steep for 5-10 minutes. Strain and drink warm. This simple tea is ideal for sipping after meals to support digestion or any time Taurus needs a cooling, refreshing break from routine.

Conclusion

The grounding herbs thyme and spearmint align harmoniously with Taurus' characteristics, providing support for their stable and practical nature while fostering flexibility. Thyme's protective and invigorating properties bolster Taurus' immune system and sense of well-being, while spearmint clears the mind and soothes the digestive system. Incorporating these herbs into daily routines can help Taurus maintain balance and comfort in their lives, allowing them to thrive in their pursuit of stability and security.

With a newfound understanding of these botanical allies, Taurus can fully embrace their earthy essence while remaining open to new possibilities. In the following chapters, we will explore more herbal alignments for the remaining zodiac signs, providing insights and practical applications to enhance the journey toward spiritual growth and well-being.

Check out my Virtual dispensary for all your hemp needs: https://shift.store/sg1fan23477/retail

Chapter 3: Gemini and Its Versatile Herbs

Gemini Features

Gemini, the third sign of the zodiac, is ruled by Mercury and embodies duality, communication, and intellectual curiosity. Symbolized by the Twins, Gemini individuals are known for their adaptability and versatile nature, effortlessly shifting between diverse interests and pursuits. As an air sign, they possess a keen intellect and are driven by a desire for mental stimulation. They are excellent communicators, often thriving in social situations where they can exchange ideas and explore new concepts.

Geminis are curious, expressive, and quick-witted, frequently juggling multiple projects or hobbies at once. This duality allows them to view situations from multiple angles, making them adept problem-solvers and negotiators. However, their constant quest for novelty can sometimes lead to a scattered focus or superficial understanding. They may struggle with indecisiveness and stress due to overcommitment. To help balance their mental energy, Gemini benefits from versatile herbs that can calm the mind, improve focus, and support their communication skills.

Herbal Alignments

Given Gemini's dynamic personality and varying needs, herbs that can both calm and invigorate are particularly valuable. The following herbs —lavender and licorice—are ideal botanical allies to help Geminis find balance, enhance their communication skills, and adapt to changing circumstances.

1. **Lavender (Lavandula angustifolia)**

   Lavender is a versatile herb that is well-suited to Gemini's multi-faceted nature. It has calming and balancing properties that soothe the nervous system, helping to alleviate stress and anxiety often associated with their busy, active minds. Its sweet fragrance promotes relaxation and enhances concentration, enabling

Gemini to remain focused and collected amid their diverse interests. Additionally, lavender is known to improve sleep quality, which can be beneficial for Geminis who may struggle to wind down at night.

Recipe - Lavender Oil for Diffusers:
- 1 cup dried lavender flowers
- 1 cup jojoba or sweet almond oil

  Combine the dried lavender flowers and oil in a clean, airtight jar. Let the mixture infuse in a warm spot for 4-6 weeks, shaking it gently every few days. Strain the oil into a glass bottle. Add a few drops of this lavender-infused oil to a diffuser to create a calming atmosphere that promotes focus and mental clarity.

2. **Licorice (Glycyrrhiza glabra)**

Licorice is another adaptable herb that complements Gemini's lively disposition. It acts as an adaptogen, helping the body manage stress and maintain equilibrium. This sweet-tasting root is also known to soothe the throat and support the respiratory system, which is crucial for Geminis who rely on their voice for effective communication. Additionally, licorice root can aid in digestion and improve energy levels.

Recipe - Licorice Root Tea:
- 1 tablespoon dried licorice root
- 2 cups water

Add the dried licorice root to a pot with water. Bring to a boil, then reduce the heat and simmer for 10 minutes. Strain and enjoy this tea warm. Its sweet and soothing taste makes it an ideal beverage for moments when Geminis need to calm their nerves, focus their minds, and strengthen their voice.

Conclusion

Lavender and licorice are two versatile herbs that resonate with Gemini's dual and communicative nature. Lavender's calming effects help

Geminis find mental balance and relaxation, while licorice enhances their adaptability and supports their respiratory health. By incorporating these herbs into their daily routines, Geminis can manage stress, improve focus, and strengthen their communication skills. In this way, they can harness the best of their innate versatility and intellectual curiosity while avoiding the pitfalls of overextending themselves.

As we continue to explore the zodiacal wheel, each chapter will provide further insights into how specific herbs can empower and balance each sign's unique attributes, guiding readers toward personal growth and spiritual alignment.

Check out my Virtual dispensary for all your hemp needs: https://shift.store/sg1fan23477/retail

Chapter 4: Cancer and Its Nurturing Herbs

Cancer Attributes

Cancer, the fourth sign of the zodiac, is ruled by the Moon and symbolizes nurturing, protection, and emotional depth. Represented by the Crab, Cancer individuals are known for their strong connection to home, family, and their emotional world. They exhibit a deep sense of empathy and intuition, often placing the needs of others before their own. Cancer thrives in environments that are supportive and secure, where they can foster meaningful relationships and provide care.

Their sensitive nature is like a tide, flowing between moments of warmth and withdrawal as they instinctively protect their vulnerabilities. This water sign is ruled by the Moon, which governs emotions, instincts, and cycles. While Cancer possesses a nurturing and compassionate spirit, they may struggle with emotional turbulence and a tendency to hold onto past hurts. They can benefit from practices that provide emotional comfort and healing, helping them maintain balance and protect their energy.

Herbal Alignments

Nurturing, soothing herbs align perfectly with Cancer's attributes, helping them find healing, comfort, and balance. Chamomile and aloe are two ideal herbs to support Cancer's protective and compassionate qualities.

1. **Chamomile (Matricaria chamomilla or Chamaemelum nobile)**
   Chamomile is renowned for its calming and anti-inflammatory

properties, which align well with Cancer's desire for nurturing comfort. It's particularly effective in reducing stress, soothing digestive discomfort, and promoting relaxation. Cancer individuals often absorb the emotions of others, which can lead to emotional overload. Chamomile's gentle sedative effects help calm the mind and improve sleep quality, while its soothing properties alleviate physical and emotional tension.

Recipe - Chamomile Bath Soak:
- ½ cup dried chamomile flowers
- ¼ cup Epsom salt
- 1 tablespoon baking soda

Mix the dried chamomile flowers, Epsom salt, and baking soda together. Add this blend to a cloth bag or tie it up in cheesecloth and place it in warm bathwater. Soak in this calming bath for 20-30 minutes, allowing chamomile's soothing effects to relax your muscles and ease emotional tension.

2. **Aloe (Aloe vera)**

Aloe is a versatile and cooling herb that is well-suited for Cancer's nurturing and protective nature. It is renowned for its healing properties, particularly in soothing burns, irritation, and inflammation. Aloe gel is rich in vitamins and antioxidants, which nourish the skin and promote overall health. For Cancer individuals who often experience emotional ups and downs, aloe provides a comforting balm to rejuvenate their spirit. It can be applied topically for skin health or ingested for digestive support.

Recipe - Aloe Vera Juice:
- 1 large aloe vera leaf
- 2 cups cold water
- 1 tablespoon honey (optional)

Cut the aloe vera leaf lengthwise and scoop out the gel into a blender. Add cold water and honey (if using) and blend until smooth. Strain to remove any fibrous bits, then chill the juice in the refrigerator. Drink a small glass daily to soothe digestion and boost your immune system.

Conclusion

Chamomile and aloe are nurturing herbs that align beautifully with Cancer's emotional and protective attributes. Chamomile's calming nature and anti-inflammatory effects help Cancer individuals find peace and relaxation, while aloe's healing and soothing properties promote skin health and rejuvenate their spirit. By incorporating these herbs into their daily self-care routines, Cancers can support their innate desire to care for others while also protecting their own well-being.

As we explore each zodiac sign and its herbal alignments, we continue to uncover the unique ways in which botanical allies can enrich spiritual growth and align with astrological energies. These insights are essential for achieving balance and living harmoniously with the rhythms of the cosmos.

Check out my Virtual dispensary for all your hemp needs: https://shift.store/sg1fan23477/retail

Chapter 5: Leo and Its Radiant Herbs

Leo Qualities

Leo, the fifth sign of the zodiac, is ruled by the Sun and symbolizes radiance, leadership, and bold self-expression. Represented by the Lion, Leo individuals are often recognized for their charismatic and dynamic personalities. They exude confidence, vitality, and a natural flair for the dramatic. As a fire sign, Leos are driven by a desire to lead and shine brightly in all their endeavors. They embrace life with an open heart, often becoming the center of attention due to their generous spirit and infectious energy.

Leos value creativity and self-expression and are drawn to pursuits where they can inspire others. Their courage and determination make them formidable leaders. However, their strong sense of pride may also lead to overconfidence or stubbornness. While they thrive on admiration and recognition, they can sometimes struggle with self-doubt when they feel unappreciated. To support their radiant personalities, Leo benefits from herbs that enhance vitality, creativity, and confidence while providing a grounding balance.

Herbal Alignments

For Leos, herbs that resonate with solar energy, vitality, and confidence are ideal botanical allies. Sunflower and saffron are two herbs that align perfectly with Leo's radiant attributes, enhancing their natural leadership qualities while also offering balance.

1. **Sunflower (Helianthus annuus)**

   Sunflower, ruled by the Sun and embodying its radiant energy, perfectly aligns with Leo's bold and positive personality. Its bright blooms symbolize joy, loyalty, and warmth, reflecting Leo's generous spirit. Sunflower seeds are rich in vitamins, minerals, and healthy fats, providing nourishment that supports Leo's active lifestyle. Sunflower oil is often used to promote healthy skin and hair, adding to their natural vitality.

Recipe - Sunflower Seed Butter:

- 2 cups sunflower seeds
- 1-2 tablespoons sunflower oil
- 1 tablespoon honey (optional)
- Salt to taste

Roast the sunflower seeds at 350°F for 10-12 minutes until golden. Once cooled, blend the seeds in a food processor until they form a smooth paste. Add sunflower oil, honey, and salt, blending again until the mixture reaches the desired consistency. Spread this vibrant sunflower seed butter on toast or add it to smoothies for a nourishing snack that supports energy and vitality.

2. **Saffron (Crocus sativus)**

Saffron, known as the "golden spice," is associated with creativity, strength, and vitality—qualities that resonate deeply with Leo. The rich, golden-red stigmas of the saffron flower have long been prized for their distinctive color and flavor. Saffron is known to improve mood and mental clarity, which is beneficial for Leos seeking to channel their creativity and leadership effectively. Additionally, its antioxidant properties can help maintain a healthy heart and skin, complementing Leo's desire for vibrancy and self-care.

Recipe - Saffron Rice:

- 1 cup basmati rice
- 2 cups water
- ¼ teaspoon saffron threads
- 2 tablespoons ghee
- Salt to taste

Rinse the rice thoroughly and soak for 20 minutes. Meanwhile, soak the saffron threads in a small bowl with warm water.

Heat ghee in a pan and sauté the rinsed rice for a few minutes. Add water, saffron threads (along with the soaking water), and salt. Bring to a boil, then reduce the heat and simmer covered for 15 minutes. Fluff with a fork and serve. This golden-hued rice is not only visually stunning but also imparts a rich flavor and positive energy that resonates with Leo's creative spirit.

Conclusion

Sunflower and saffron are radiant herbs that align beautifully with Leo's confident and bold attributes. Sunflower provides nourishment and vitality that fuel Leos' active lifestyle, while saffron enhances their creativity and leadership qualities. Incorporating these herbs into their diets can help Leos remain grounded while shining brightly in all their pursuits.

As we continue exploring the zodiac wheel, each chapter reveals more about how specific herbs can empower and balance each sign's unique attributes. Understanding these herbal alignments offers a holistic approach to personal growth and spiritual alignment that enables each individual to live harmoniously with their astrological nature.

Check out my Virtual dispensary for all your hemp needs: https://shift.store/sg1fan23477/retail

Chapter 6: Virgo and Its Purifying Herbs

Virgo Traits

Virgo, the sixth sign of the zodiac, is ruled by Mercury and represents meticulousness, analysis, and health-conscious living. Symbolized by the Maiden, Virgo individuals are known for their detail-oriented nature and logical approach to life. They exhibit a strong desire for order and organization, often applying their analytical skills to solve complex problems efficiently. Their innate curiosity and practical mindset drive them to seek knowledge and perfection in their pursuits.

Virgos are often drawn to health and wellness, taking great care to maintain both their physical and mental well-being. They are highly attuned to their environment and are diligent in creating routines that foster productivity. While their analytical nature makes them capable problem-solvers, it may also lead to overthinking, self-criticism, and perfectionism. To support their meticulous and health-conscious nature, Virgos benefit from purifying herbs that cleanse the body, boost immunity, and alleviate stress.

Herbal Alignments

Herbs that provide cleansing and healing properties align well with Virgo's traits, helping them maintain purity, clarity, and balance. Fennel and echinacea are two herbs that align perfectly with Virgo's health-focused tendencies.

1. **Fennel (Foeniculum vulgare)**

   Fennel, a sweet and aromatic herb, has long been recognized for its purifying and digestive benefits. It is often used to alleviate bloating, indigestion, and discomfort, helping Virgos maintain optimal digestion, which is crucial given their health-conscious mindset. Fennel seeds contain antioxidants and essential oils that cleanse the body and support liver function. Additionally, fennel's calming properties help ease stress and promote mental clarity, aiding Virgos in their analytical pursuits.

Recipe - Fennel Digestive Tea:
- 1 teaspoon fennel seeds
- 1 cup boiling water
- 1 teaspoon honey (optional)

Lightly crush the fennel seeds to release their oils, then place them in a cup. Pour boiling water over the seeds and steep for 10 minutes. Strain and add honey if desired. This digestive tea helps soothe the stomach, ease bloating, and refresh the mind, making it an ideal beverage after meals or during moments of stress.

2. **Echinacea (Echinacea purpurea)**

Echinacea, known for its immune-boosting properties, is a powerful ally for Virgo's health-conscious mindset. It stimulates the immune system to fight off infections and promotes detoxification, making it a valuable herb during seasonal changes or when the immune system needs a boost. Its antioxidant properties support the body's natural defenses while reducing inflammation, providing holistic support for Virgo's pursuit of well-being.

Recipe - Echinacea Immune Tonic:
- 1 tablespoon dried echinacea root
- 1 tablespoon dried elderberries
- 2 cups water
- 1 tablespoon honey

Combine the echinacea root, elderberries, and water in a pot and bring to a boil. Reduce heat and simmer for 20 minutes. Strain, then stir in honey while the liquid is still warm. Store in a glass jar in the refrigerator. Take a spoonful daily or add to herbal teas to fortify the immune system and cleanse the body.

promoting emotional harmony. Its antioxidant properties also support skin health, contributing to Libra's appreciation for beauty and self-care.

Recipe - Rose Petal Infusion:
- 1 tablespoon dried rose petals
- 1 cup boiling water
- 1 teaspoon honey (optional)

Place the dried rose petals in a cup and pour boiling water over them. Cover and steep for 10-15 minutes. Strain and add honey if desired. This delicate infusion can be sipped in the morning or evening to bring balance and peace, promoting Libra's harmonious approach to life.

2. **Peppermint (Mentha piperita)**

Peppermint is a refreshing and stimulating herb that helps Libra maintain mental clarity and focus. It alleviates fatigue and indigestion, both of which may occur when Libras overextend themselves. Peppermint's cooling properties reduce stress and tension, promoting a clear mind and restoring balance to Libra's often busy schedule.

Recipe - Peppermint and Lemon Balm Iced Tea:
- 1 tablespoon dried peppermint leaves
- 1 tablespoon dried lemon balm leaves
- 4 cups boiling water
- 1 lemon, sliced
- Ice cubes

Combine the dried peppermint and lemon balm leaves in a teapot. Pour boiling water over the herbs and steep for 10-15 minutes. Strain and let the tea cool to room temperature. Serve over ice with a slice of lemon for a refreshing, balancing beverage that enhances mental clarity and refreshes the spirit.

Conclusion

Rose and peppermint are balancing herbs that align beautifully with

Libra's harmonious and gracious essence. Rose promotes emotional harmony and peace, while peppermint provides mental clarity and invigoration. Incorporating these herbs into their routines can help Libras maintain equilibrium, gracefully navigating their relationships and decisions.

As we progress through the zodiac wheel, each chapter continues to explore how specific herbs resonate with the distinctive characteristics of each sign. Understanding these alignments offers readers holistic practices that empower them to live harmoniously with their astrological nature while cultivating personal growth and spiritual alignment.

Check out my Virtual dispensary for all your hemp needs: https://shift.store/sg1fan23477/retail

Chapter 8: Scorpio and Its Intensive Herbs

Scorpio Features

Scorpio, the eighth sign of the zodiac, is ruled by both Mars and Pluto and symbolizes intensity, transformation, and depth. Represented by the Scorpion, Scorpio individuals are known for their strong willpower, keen intuition, and profound emotional depth. They approach life with an unwavering focus, seeking out deeper truths and reveling in the power of transformation. Scorpios thrive in pursuits that challenge them to explore the mysteries of life, often drawn to psychology, esotericism, and other fields that probe the depths of human existence.

Despite their intensity, Scorpios maintain an air of mystery and often guard their vulnerabilities closely. They are fiercely loyal to those they trust and hold deep convictions. However, their passion and determination can sometimes lead to over-commitment, possessiveness, or mistrust. To support their transformative processes and emotional resilience, Scorpios benefit from herbs that resonate with their intense energy and stimulate healing and renewal.

Herbal Alignments

Herbs that are potent, purifying, and transformative align well with Scorpio's intense nature. Garlic and ginger are two herbs that reflect Scorpio's depth, promoting internal cleansing and emotional transformation.

1. **Garlic (Allium sativum)**

   Garlic is a powerful herb known for its purifying, antibacterial, and immune-boosting properties. Its pungent aroma and flavor embody Scorpio's intensity, while its medicinal benefits align with Scorpio's need for internal transformation and resilience. Garlic stimulates circulation, supports digestion, and helps detoxify the body. Its warming effects promote circulation, which aligns with Scorpio's fiery energy and enhances their transformative processes.

Recipe - Garlic Tonic:
- 1 garlic bulb, peeled and minced
- 1 cup apple cider vinegar
- 1 tablespoon honey
- 1 teaspoon cayenne pepper

Combine the minced garlic, apple cider vinegar, honey, and cayenne pepper in a glass jar. Seal the jar and let the mixture infuse for at least two weeks, shaking it daily. Strain the tonic into a clean bottle and store it in the refrigerator. Take a teaspoon daily to strengthen the immune system and detoxify the body.

2. **Ginger (Zingiber officinale)**

Ginger is a stimulating herb that enhances circulation, improves digestion, and warms the body. Its spicy flavor and penetrating effects reflect Scorpio's transformative qualities, providing the fire needed to ignite change and release blockages. Ginger also possesses anti-inflammatory properties, helping to alleviate physical discomfort and soothe emotional tension. It is particularly beneficial for Scorpios experiencing stagnation or seeking to renew their energy.

Recipe - Ginger Elixir:
- 1-inch fresh ginger root, peeled and sliced
- 2 cups water
- 1 tablespoon honey
- Juice of half a lemon

Add the sliced ginger root to a pot with water and bring to a boil. Reduce heat and simmer for 10 minutes. Strain the liquid into a cup, then stir in honey and lemon juice. This warming elixir stimulates circulation and digestion, promoting renewal and clarity.

Conclusion

Garlic and ginger are intensive herbs that align perfectly with Scorpio's transformative nature. Garlic's immune-boosting and purifying effects help Scorpios cleanse and renew their energy, while ginger's stimulating properties promote circulation and help them embrace change. Incorporating these herbs into their routines can support Scorpios in their pursuit of depth, intensity, and transformation.

As we journey through the zodiac wheel, each chapter reveals how specific herbs can align with the distinct attributes of each sign. Understanding these alignments allows readers to cultivate holistic practices that harmonize with their astrological nature and guide them toward personal growth and spiritual transformation.

Check out my Virtual dispensary for all your hemp needs: https://shift.store/sg1fan23477/retail

Chapter 9: Sagittarius and Its Expansive Herbs

Sagittarius Traits

Sagittarius, the ninth sign of the zodiac, is ruled by Jupiter and represents expansion, exploration, and optimism. Symbolized by the Archer, Sagittarius individuals are known for their adventurous spirit and love of freedom. They are natural-born explorers who eagerly seek new experiences, knowledge, and understanding of the world around them. With an open mind and a generous heart, Sagittarians approach life with positivity and enthusiasm, always striving to broaden their horizons.

As a fire sign, Sagittarius embodies dynamic energy, constantly pursuing growth and independence. They are fascinated by philosophy, spirituality, and cultural diversity. However, their love for freedom and exploration can sometimes make them restless, impatient, or prone to overindulgence. To support their adventurous and expansive nature, Sagittarians benefit from herbs that promote growth, creativity, and resilience, helping them stay grounded while nurturing their desire for exploration.

Herbal Alignments

Herbs that stimulate creativity and support spiritual growth align well with Sagittarius's expansive spirit. Sage and turmeric are two herbs that complement Sagittarius's optimistic outlook and adventurous nature, encouraging clarity, insight, and exploration.

1. **Sage (Salvia officinalis)**

   Sage, with its name derived from the Latin "salvare," meaning "to heal," is a revered herb known for its wisdom-enhancing and clarifying properties. It is often associated with spiritual growth and mental clarity, making it an ideal ally for Sagittarius. Its earthy aroma and warming effects help promote insight and focus, aligning with Sagittarius's quest for knowledge and expansion. Additionally, sage's antioxidant and antimicrobial properties support overall health and well-being.

Recipe - Sage Smudge Stick:
- A handful of dried sage leaves
- Cotton string or thread

Bundle the dried sage leaves together and secure them with the string, tightly wrapping it around the bundle. Allow the bundle to dry completely before use. Light the end of the smudge stick and allow it to smolder. Use the smoke to cleanse your space or body, promoting spiritual growth, insight, and positivity.

2. **Turmeric (Curcuma longa)**

Turmeric, with its rich golden color and earthy flavor, is known for its powerful anti-inflammatory and antioxidant properties. It aligns perfectly with Sagittarius's expansive nature, promoting growth, vitality, and resilience. Its active compound, curcumin, helps reduce inflammation, improve digestion, and enhance cognitive function, all of which can support Sagittarians in their pursuit of exploration and new experiences. Additionally, turmeric promotes spiritual clarity, helping Sagittarius maintain a positive outlook.

Recipe - Golden Milk:
- 1 teaspoon ground turmeric
- 1 teaspoon ground cinnamon
- 1-inch fresh ginger root, peeled and grated
- 2 cups coconut or almond milk
- 1 tablespoon honey
- Pinch of black pepper

Combine the turmeric, cinnamon, ginger, and milk in a saucepan and bring to a gentle simmer. Stir in the honey and black pepper, then simmer for 5 minutes. Strain into a cup and enjoy this warm, golden beverage that soothes the body and mind while promoting clarity and growth.

Conclusion

Sage and turmeric are expansive herbs that align beautifully with Sagittarius's adventurous and freedom-loving nature. Sage promotes insight and spiritual growth, while turmeric encourages resilience, health, and vitality. Incorporating these herbs into their routines can help Sagittarians remain grounded while exploring the world with enthusiasm and positivity.

As we move forward in the zodiac wheel, each chapter reveals how specific herbs align with the distinctive traits of each sign. By understanding these botanical alignments, readers can cultivate practices that harmonize with their astrological energies, promoting personal growth and spiritual expansion.

Check out my Virtual dispensary for all your hemp needs: https://shift.store/sg1fan23477/retail

Chapter 10: Capricorn and Its Structuring Herbs

Capricorn Attributes

Capricorn, the tenth sign of the zodiac, is ruled by Saturn and symbolizes discipline, ambition, and structure. Represented by the Sea-Goat, Capricorn individuals are known for their practicality and strong work ethic. They approach their goals with methodical planning and strategic vision, steadily climbing the metaphorical mountain toward achievement and success. Capricorns are resourceful, self-reliant, and naturally inclined to lead, often finding themselves in positions of responsibility.

As an earth sign, Capricorn is grounded, pragmatic, and rooted in reality. They value tradition, loyalty, and hard work, but their disciplined approach can sometimes lead to rigidity or overworking themselves. To support their drive for achievement and need for structure, Capricorns benefit from herbs that promote resilience, stability, and endurance.

Herbal Alignments

Herbs that are fortifying and structuring align well with Capricorn's disciplined and ambitious nature. Comfrey and vetiver are two herbs that resonate perfectly with Capricorn's grounded qualities, promoting stability and strength.

1. **Comfrey (Symphytum officinale)**

   Comfrey, known as the "knitbone," is a deeply healing and restorative herb. Its mucilaginous and anti-inflammatory properties help repair damaged tissues, making it invaluable for healing injuries and enhancing resilience. Comfrey's ability to restore and strengthen aligns with Capricorn's ambition and desire for success. Whether used externally or internally (with caution due to potential toxicity), comfrey supports the body's structure and fosters healing and renewal.

Recipe - Comfrey Salve:
- 1 cup dried comfrey leaves
- 1 cup olive oil
- 1 ounce beeswax pellets
- 10 drops tea tree oil (optional)

Infuse the dried comfrey leaves in olive oil for two weeks in a warm, sunny spot. Strain the oil and place it in a double boiler with the beeswax pellets. Heat gently until the beeswax is fully melted, then stir in the tea tree oil. Pour the mixture into a glass jar and let it cool. Apply this salve to sprains, bruises, and sore muscles to promote healing and resilience.

2. **Vetiver (Chrysopogon zizanioides)**

Vetiver, a perennial grass, is known for its grounding and stabilizing properties. Its earthy aroma aligns perfectly with Capricorn's pragmatic qualities, promoting a sense of rootedness and calm. Vetiver's ability to support emotional resilience and stability helps Capricorns stay centered while navigating their ambitious pursuits. Its essential oil is often used in aromatherapy to relieve stress, improve focus, and promote restful sleep.

Recipe - Vetiver and Lavender Bath Soak:
- 1 cup Epsom salt
- 10 drops vetiver essential oil
- 10 drops lavender essential oil

Mix the Epsom salt with the vetiver and lavender essential oils in a bowl. Stir well, then store the mixture in a glass jar. Add a handful to warm bathwater and soak for 20 minutes to release tension, ground your energy, and restore calm.

Conclusion

Comfrey and vetiver are structuring herbs that align well with Capricorn's disciplined and ambitious nature. Comfrey's restorative properties strengthen and heal, while vetiver's grounding effects stabilize and calm the mind. Incorporating these herbs into their routines can help Capricorns build a solid foundation, supporting their path toward success and accomplishment.

As we continue exploring the zodiac wheel, each chapter reveals how specific herbs can resonate with and empower the unique characteristics of each sign. Understanding these botanical alignments allows readers to cultivate holistic practices that harmonize with their astrological energies, fostering personal growth and achievement.

Check out my Virtual dispensary for all your hemp needs: https://shift.store/sg1fan23477/retail

Chapter 11: Aquarius and Its Innovative Herbs
Aquarius Qualities

Aquarius, the eleventh sign of the zodiac, is ruled by Uranus and represents innovation, progressiveness, and unconventional thinking. Symbolized by the Water Bearer, Aquarius individuals are known for their visionary ideas, humanitarian spirit, and open-minded nature. They challenge traditional norms, constantly seeking new ways to improve society and advance technology. Aquarians are natural problem-solvers, eager to share their unique perspectives and challenge the status quo.

As an air sign, Aquarius thrives on intellectual stimulation, valuing individuality and diversity of thought. They possess a strong desire for freedom and often find comfort in unconventional settings or lifestyles. However, their innovative mindset and love for new ideas can sometimes make them emotionally detached or overly idealistic. To support their inventive and progressive spirit, Aquarians benefit from herbs that stimulate mental clarity, creativity, and relaxation, helping them remain focused while fostering their innovative potential.

Herbal Alignments

Herbs that promote creativity, clarity, and unconventional thinking align well with Aquarius's innovative and progressive nature. Kava and ginkgo are two herbs that resonate with Aquarius's unique energy, stimulating mental activity and innovation.

1. **Kava (Piper methysticum)**
   Kava, a root native to the South Pacific, is known for its calming and anxiety-reducing effects. It has been traditionally used

in ceremonial contexts to promote relaxation and enhance social interactions. Kava's ability to reduce stress and encourage creativity aligns perfectly with Aquarius's desire for intellectual freedom and clarity. Its calming properties help Aquarians ground themselves in the present moment, allowing their minds to roam freely.

Recipe - Kava Drink:

- 1 cup kava powder
- 4 cups water
- 1 teaspoon coconut oil
- Sweetener (optional)

In a blender, combine the kava powder and water. Blend on high for 4-5 minutes. Strain the mixture through a muslin cloth or fine sieve into a bowl, then stir in the coconut oil and sweetener if desired. Sip this calming beverage to relax the mind, stimulate creativity, and open yourself to new ideas.

2. **Ginkgo (Ginkgo biloba)**

Ginkgo, one of the oldest living tree species, is known for its cognitive-enhancing and memory-boosting effects. It improves blood flow to the brain, enhancing mental clarity and focus. This aligns beautifully with Aquarius's inventive nature, as it promotes mental sharpness and supports unconventional thinking. Ginkgo also has antioxidant properties, which help reduce inflammation and protect cognitive health.

Recipe - Ginkgo Tonic:

- 2 teaspoons dried ginkgo leaves
- 2 cups boiling water
- 1 teaspoon honey
- Lemon wedge

Place the dried ginkgo leaves in a teapot and pour the boiling water over them. Steep for 10-15 minutes, then strain into a cup. Add honey and a lemon wedge if desired. This tonic stimulates cognitive function, enhances creativity, and helps Aquarius unlock new perspectives.

Conclusion

Kava and ginkgo are innovative herbs that align well with Aquarius's unconventional and inventive nature. Kava's calming effects reduce stress and stimulate creativity, while ginkgo's cognitive-enhancing properties sharpen mental clarity and promote new ways of thinking. Incorporating these herbs into their routines can help Aquarians stay focused while harnessing their full imaginative potential.

Each chapter continues to explore how herbs align with the unique qualities of each zodiac sign. Understanding these botanical alignments empowers readers to create holistic practices that resonate with their astrological energies, unlocking new levels of personal growth and creativity.

Check out my Virtual dispensary for all your hemp needs: https://shift.store/sg1fan23477/retail

Chapter 12: Pisces and Its Soothing Herbs

Pisces Features

Pisces, the twelfth and final sign of the zodiac, is ruled by Neptune and embodies empathy, intuition, and creativity. Represented by the Fish, Pisces individuals are known for their deep emotional understanding, vivid imagination, and compassionate nature. They are naturally attuned to the energies of the world around them and often feel a deep spiritual connection to others. Pisceans are drawn to creative pursuits that allow them to express their emotions, often excelling in the arts.

As a water sign, Pisces is fluid, adaptable, and receptive, effortlessly flowing between different states of mind and emotion. They are highly intuitive and often operate on a more subconscious level. However, their sensitivity and dreamlike tendencies can sometimes make them prone to escapism or overwhelm. To support their empathetic and creative nature, Pisceans benefit from herbs that promote emotional healing, relaxation, and spiritual growth.

Herbal Alignments

Herbs that are soothing, intuitive, and fluid align well with Pisces's empathetic and dreamy qualities. Lotus and seaweed are two herbs that embody the gentle, healing nature of Pisces, providing emotional comfort and spiritual alignment.

1. **Lotus (Nelumbo nucifera)**

   Lotus is a sacred plant in many cultures, symbolizing purity, enlightenment, and spiritual awakening. It aligns beautifully with

Pisces's intuitive and spiritual nature, promoting calmness, creativity, and insight. The petals and seeds of the lotus plant are used to reduce anxiety, improve circulation, and promote restful sleep. Lotus can help Pisceans balance their emotions, providing tranquility amid the waves of their deep feelings.

Recipe - Lotus Tea:
- 2 teaspoons dried lotus petals or seeds
- 2 cups boiling water
- 1 teaspoon honey (optional)

Place the dried lotus petals or seeds in a teapot and pour the boiling water over them. Let steep for 10-15 minutes, then strain into a cup. Add honey if desired. This calming tea relaxes the mind and encourages creative thinking while supporting emotional well-being.

2. **Seaweed (Various species)**

Seaweed, which thrives in the ocean's depths, is rich in nutrients and aligns well with Pisces's fluid nature. It is known for its detoxifying properties and ability to nourish the body with essential minerals. Consuming seaweed can support Pisceans by replenishing their energy and enhancing their emotional resilience. Its anti-inflammatory and antioxidant properties also promote a sense of healing and renewal, helping Pisces stay grounded in their intuitive pursuits.

Recipe - Seaweed Salad:
- 1 cup dried wakame seaweed
- 1 tablespoon rice vinegar
- 1 tablespoon soy sauce
- 1 tablespoon sesame oil
- 1 teaspoon sesame seeds

Soak the dried seaweed in warm water for 10 minutes, then drain and chop into bite-sized pieces. In a bowl, mix the rice vinegar, soy sauce, and sesame oil. Add the chopped seaweed

Each chapter demonstrates how pairing zodiac signs with complementary herbs can help individuals realize their potential, work through challenges, and remain aligned with their astrological energy.

Personalization

While each zodiac sign has distinctive traits and characteristics, every individual's astrological chart is unique. Analyzing the personal planets and houses can reveal even deeper insights into the ways different herbs can complement one's needs.

For instance, a Libra individual with a strong Virgo influence in their natal chart may also benefit from herbs that are purifying and promote meticulous focus. Similarly, a Cancer with a significant Aries presence might find energetic herbs helpful for nurturing both empathy and assertiveness.

Readers are encouraged to explore their own birth charts to identify their rising, sun, moon, and other significant planetary placements. With these insights, they can create personalized herbal routines that reflect the diverse aspects of their astrological profiles.

Continued Exploration

Astrological herbalism is an expansive and evolving field that invites continuous learning and experimentation. Here are some ways to further explore:

1. **Experiment with Formulas**: Mix and match herbs to create teas, tinctures, and aromatherapy blends that align with specific planets, houses, or astrological transits.
2. **Study Historical Texts**: Dive into the writings of herbalists and astrologers from various cultures to understand traditional associations between plants and the zodiac.
3. **Keep a Journal**: Track herbal and astrological observations to identify patterns in your responses to specific herbal remedies and planetary influences.

4. **Connect with Practitioners**: Seek guidance from experienced herbalists, astrologers, or holistic health practitioners who specialize in this field.

The journey of astrological herbalism is both deeply personal and transformative. By aligning plants and planets, readers can tap into ancient wisdom and craft personalized wellness practices that are as unique as the stars themselves.

Appendix A: Herbal Preparations and Safety
Preparation Techniques

Herbal preparations vary widely, offering multiple ways to incorporate their benefits into daily life. Here are instructions for some common preparation methods:

1. **Teas (Infusions and Decoctions):**

   - **Infusions:** Best for leaves, flowers, and other delicate plant parts. Pour boiling water over the herb (1-2 teaspoons per cup of water) in a teapot or infuser. Steep for 10-15 minutes, strain, and enjoy.
   - **Decoctions:** Best for roots, bark, and seeds. Simmer 1-2 tablespoons of herbs in water for 15-30 minutes, then strain. This longer, heat-intensive process helps extract beneficial compounds from tougher plant parts.

2. **Tinctures:**

   Tinctures involve extracting herbal constituents with alcohol or glycerin.

   - **Alcohol-Based:** Combine chopped fresh or dried herbs (1:4 ratio) with high-proof alcohol. Store in a glass jar, shake daily, and let sit for 4-6 weeks. Strain through a cheesecloth or fine sieve and store in dropper bottles.
   - **Glycerin-Based:** Replace alcohol with food-grade vegetable glycerin, and follow the same procedure. Glycerin tinctures are gentler and suitable for children or those avoiding alcohol.

3. **Poultices and Compresses:**

   Poultices and compresses involve applying herbs directly to the skin for localized relief.

- ° **Poultices:** Crush or grind fresh herbs into a paste. Wrap the paste in clean cheesecloth and apply it to the affected area. Secure with a bandage or plastic wrap.
- ° **Compresses:** Steep dried or fresh herbs in hot water, then soak a clean cloth in the infusion. Apply to the affected area for 15-20 minutes.

4. **Salves and Ointments:**

These semi-solid preparations are perfect for skin issues and topical application.

- ° Melt beeswax or a vegetable-based solid oil (e.g., coconut oil) in a double boiler.
- ° Add an infused oil (or combination of oils) to the mixture and stir.
- ° Pour into small glass jars and let cool before sealing. Essential oils can also be added for fragrance or additional benefits.

Safety Guidelines

While herbs offer powerful benefits, their potency also requires careful usage. Follow these guidelines to ensure safe herbal practices:

1. **Dosage and Duration:**

- ° Begin with small doses and gradually increase, watching for any adverse reactions.
- ° Avoid prolonged use of certain herbs without breaks, as tolerance or toxicity may develop over time.
- ° Herbal teas should generally be consumed up to 3 cups a day, while tinctures are taken in small amounts (1-2 dropperfuls).

2. **Interactions:**

- Some herbs may interact with prescription medications, such as blood thinners or antidepressants. Consult a healthcare provider if you are taking any medications or have existing health conditions.
- Avoid using certain herbs during pregnancy or while breastfeeding unless advised by a professional.

3. **Quality and Sourcing:**

- Purchase herbs from reputable suppliers, ensuring they are organic, non-GMO, and ethically sourced.
- When wild-harvesting, ensure the plants are not endangered, and only take what you need without harming the environment.

4. **Identification and Allergies:**

- Properly identify wild plants before use. Mistaking one species for another can result in unintended side effects.
- Conduct a patch test to check for skin allergies before applying an herbal preparation.

Conclusion

Understanding preparation techniques and safety guidelines is crucial for safely harnessing the power of herbs. By incorporating these practices into your routine, you can create herbal preparations that are both effective and tailored to your needs. This appendix serves as a foundation for further exploration into the practical side of herbalism, empowering you to craft and enjoy botanical remedies that align with your unique astrological energies.

Appendix B: Astrology for Beginners
Foundations

Astrology offers a rich tapestry of symbols and patterns, linking the movements of celestial bodies to human experiences. To explore how astrological energies impact herbal alignments, let's understand the fundamental components: signs, planets, houses, and aspects.

1. **Signs**

   The zodiac signs represent twelve distinct personality archetypes and energies. Each sign falls into one of four elements (fire, earth, air, water) and three qualities (cardinal, fixed, mutable). Here's a brief overview of each sign:
   - **Aries**: Bold, pioneering, and energetic (fire, cardinal)
   - **Taurus**: Grounded, patient, and determined (earth, fixed)
   - **Gemini**: Adaptable, curious, and communicative (air, mutable)
   - **Cancer**: Nurturing, intuitive, and protective (water, cardinal)
   - **Leo**: Confident, generous, and dramatic (fire, fixed)
   - **Virgo**: Analytical, meticulous, and health-oriented (earth, mutable)
   - **Libra**: Harmonious, diplomatic, and fair-minded (air, cardinal)

- **Scorpio**: Intense, transformative, and resourceful (water, fixed)
- **Sagittarius**: Adventurous, philosophical, and optimistic (fire, mutable)
- **Capricorn**: Disciplined, ambitious, and pragmatic (earth, cardinal)
- **Aquarius**: Innovative, unconventional, and humanitarian (air, fixed)
- **Pisces**: Compassionate, intuitive, and artistic (water, mutable)

2. Planets

Each planet governs different aspects of personality and behavior, reflecting specific energies that affect how we interact with the world. The planets can be broadly categorized as:

- **Personal Planets**: Sun (self), Moon (emotions), Mercury (intellect), Venus (love), and Mars (drive).
- **Social Planets**: Jupiter (expansion) and Saturn (discipline).
- **Transpersonal Planets**: Uranus (innovation), Neptune (spirituality), and Pluto (transformation).

3. Houses

Astrological houses represent different life areas or experiences, with twelve houses dividing the zodiac wheel. The first house begins with the Ascendant (rising sign), reflecting one's outward persona. Key houses include:

- **1st House (Self)**: Identity and outward personality.
- **4th House (Home)**: Family, ancestry, and emotional foundation.
- **7th House (Partnerships)**: Relationships, both romantic and professional.
- **10th House (Career)**: Public image, career, and social status.

4. **Aspects**

Aspects are the angular relationships between planets, affecting how they interact. Major aspects include:

- **Conjunction (0°):** Amplifies the combined energy of two planets.
- **Opposition (180°):** Creates tension, highlighting opposing influences.
- **Trine (120°):** Harmonious, indicating a smooth flow between planets.
- **Square (90°):** Creates friction, demanding resolution or action.

Interpretation

Interpreting an astrological chart helps identify how planetary energies influence various aspects of life. Here are tips for tailoring herbal choices to individual alignments:

1. **Identify the Sun, Moon, and Rising Signs:**
   - The Sun sign indicates core personality traits and aspirations.
   - The Moon sign reveals emotional needs and responses.
   - The Rising (Ascendant) sign reflects outward behavior and how others perceive you.
     For example, a Leo Sun individual may be drawn to herbs that promote confidence, while a Virgo Moon may benefit from purifying herbs.

2. **Analyze Personal Planets:**
   Look at the placement of Mercury, Venus, and Mars to understand intellectual preferences, love language, and drive. For instance, someone with Mercury in Gemini may prefer versatile herbs that support mental agility.

3. **Assess House Placements:**
   Examine the houses to understand the planetary influences on

specific life areas. For example, if the 6th House of health contains Venus, consider soothing herbs that nurture both beauty and well-being.

4. **Consider Aspects**:
   Review major aspects between planets for insights into how different energies interact. A challenging Mars square Saturn aspect may benefit from herbs that soothe frustration and help set achievable goals.

By understanding these astrological fundamentals and applying them to individual charts, readers can develop personalized herbal practices that align with their celestial energies. The intricate dance between planets, signs, houses, and aspects provides a cosmic guide, empowering individuals to create herbal routines that resonate with their unique astrological blueprint.

<u>Message from the Author:</u>

I hope you enjoyed this book, I love astrology and knew there was not a book such as this out on the shelf. I love metaphysical items as well. Please check out my other books:

-Life of Government Benefits

-My life of Hell

-My life with Hydrocephalus

-Red Sky

-World Domination:Woman's rule

-World Domination:Woman's Rule 2: The War

-Life and Banishment of Apophis: book 1

-The Kidney Friendly Diet

-The Ultimate Hemp Cookbook

-Creating a Dispensary(legally)

-Cleanliness throughout life: the importance of showering from childhood to adulthood.

-Strong Roots: The Risks of Overcoddling children

-Hemp Horoscopes: Cosmic Insights and Earthly Healing

- Celestial Hemp Navigating the Zodiac: Through the Green Cosmos

-Astrological Hemp: Aligning The Stars with Earth's Ancient Herb

-The Astrological Guide to Hemp: Stars, Signs, and Sacred Leaves

-Green Growth: Innovative Marketing Strategies for your Hemp Products and Dispensary

-Cosmic Cannabis

-Astrological Munchies

-Henry The Hemp

-Zodiacal Roots: The Astrological Soul Of Hemp

- **Green Constellations: Intersection of Hemp and Zodiac**

-Hemp in The Houses: An astrological Adventure Through The Cannabis Galaxy

-Galactic Ganja Guide

Heavenly Hemp
Zodiac Leaves
Doctor Who Astrology
Cannastrology
Stellar Satvias and Cosmic Indicas
Celestial Cannabis: A Zodiac Journey
AstroHerbology: The Sky and The Soil: Volume 1
AstroHerbology:Celestial Cannabis:Volume 2
Cosmic Cannabis Cultivation
The Starry Guide to Herbal Harmony: Volume 1
The Starry Guide to Herbal Harmony: Cannabis Universe: Volume 2
Yugioh Astrology: Astrological Guide to Deck, Duels and more
Nightmare Mansion: Echoes of The Abyss
Nightmare Mansion 2: Legacy of Shadows
Nightmare Mansion 3: Shadows of the Forgotten
Nightmare Mansion 4: Echoes of the Damned
The Life and Banishment of Apophis: Book 2
Nightmare Mansion: Halls of Despair
Healing with Herb: Cannabis and Hydrocephalus
Planetary Pot: Aligning with Astrological Herbs: Volume 1
Fast Track to Freedom: 30 Days to Financial Independence Using AI, Assets, and Agile Hustles
Cosmic Hemp Pathways
How to Become Financially Free in 30 Days: 10,000 Paths to Prosperity

Check out my Virtual dispensary for all your hemp needs: https://shift.store/sg1fan23477/retail

If you want solar for your home go here: https://www.harborsolar.live/apophisenterprises/

Instagrams:
@apophis_enterprises,
@hempkingdom2024,
@apophisbookemporium,
@apophisfashion,
@apophisscardshop
Twitter: @apophisenterpr1,
Tiktok:@apophisenterprise
Youtube: @sg1fan23477
Podcast:Apophis Chat Zone: https://open.spotify.com/show/5zXbrCLEV2xzCp8ybrfHsk?si=fb4d4fdbdce44dec
Newsletter: https://apophiss-newsletter-27c897.beehiiv.com/

and toss to coat. Sprinkle sesame seeds on top. This salad is a light, refreshing way to enjoy seaweed's nourishing properties while supporting intuitive clarity and grounding.

Conclusion

Lotus and seaweed are soothing herbs that align perfectly with Pisces's empathetic and dreamy characteristics. Lotus promotes emotional balance and insight, while seaweed nourishes the body and provides grounding. Incorporating these herbs into their routines can help Pisceans find tranquility in their emotional depths and embrace their creative potential.

Each chapter of the zodiac wheel has revealed how specific herbs can resonate with and empower the unique traits of each sign. By understanding these botanical alignments, readers can cultivate holistic practices that harmonize with their astrological energies, guiding them on a journey of personal growth, spiritual awakening, and creativity.

Check out my Virtual dispensary for all your hemp needs: https://shift.store/sg1fan23477/retail

Conclusion: Personalizing Your Herbal Journey
Recap

Throughout *Zodiacal Herbage: Astrological Insights: Volume 1*, we have explored how specific herbs resonate with and empower each zodiac sign's unique qualities. Each chapter provides insights into how herbal alignments can support personal growth, health, and spiritual development.

- **Aries** was paired with energetic herbs like nettle and basil to fuel the fiery, pioneering spirit.
- **Taurus** benefited from grounding herbs such as thyme and spearmint to nurture stability and comfort.
- **Gemini** embraced versatile herbs like lavender and licorice to enhance its communicative and adaptable nature.
- **Cancer** found emotional support and healing through nurturing herbs like chamomile and aloe.
- **Leo** thrived with radiant herbs like sunflower and saffron that amplified its bold and vital energy.
- **Virgo** relied on purifying herbs like fennel and echinacea to support meticulous health-focused tendencies.
- **Libra** discovered balance and harmony through rose and peppermint, which promote inner calm and equilibrium.
- **Scorpio** aligned with deep, penetrating herbs like garlic and ginger to match its transformative power.
- **Sagittarius** expanded horizons with sage and turmeric to encourage growth and exploration.
- **Capricorn** structured its ambitions with the resilience-enhancing properties of comfrey and vetiver.
- **Aquarius** stimulated innovation and creativity with kava and ginkgo, perfectly suited to its unconventional nature.
- **Pisces** embraced the calming and healing properties of lotus and seaweed, enhancing its empathetic and intuitive spirit.

Chapter 7: Libra and Its Balancing Herbs
Libra Characteristics

Libra, the seventh sign of the zodiac, is ruled by Venus and represents harmony, balance, and relationships. Symbolized by the Scales, Libra individuals are known for their diplomatic and gracious nature, often striving to create equilibrium in their lives and the lives of others. They are naturally drawn to beauty, fairness, and collaboration, preferring environments that are peaceful and aesthetically pleasing. Their strong social skills make them excellent mediators, always seeking to resolve conflicts amicably.

As an air sign, Libra values intellectual stimulation and enjoys engaging in thoughtful discussions. They are inclined to explore ideas and perspectives to understand the world around them better. However, their strong desire for balance can sometimes result in indecision or avoidance, as they strive to make the best choice possible. They benefit from practices that promote calmness, clarity, and self-confidence to maintain their sense of balance and well-being.

Herbal Alignments

Herbs that promote calmness and emotional balance are ideal for Libra, helping them remain grounded while embracing their diplomatic and harmonious spirit. Rose and peppermint are two herbs that align well with Libra's balancing essence.

1. **Rose (Rosa spp.)**

   Rose is known for its gentle, soothing, and heart-healing properties. Ruled by Venus, it embodies the themes of love, beauty, and balance, making it an ideal ally for Libra. Rose petals have a calming effect on the nervous system, reducing anxiety and

Conclusion

Fennel and echinacea are purifying herbs that align beautifully with Virgo's meticulous and health-focused tendencies. Fennel's digestive and calming properties support Virgos in maintaining physical and mental balance, while echinacea's immune-boosting effects ensure they remain fortified and resilient. By incorporating these herbs into their daily routines, Virgos can enhance their pursuit of purity, clarity, and well-being.

As we continue our journey through the zodiac, each chapter uncovers more about how specific herbs empower and align with the distinct qualities of each sign. By understanding these botanical connections, readers can create holistic practices that harmonize with their unique astrological energies and personal growth goals.

Check out my Virtual dispensary for all your hemp needs: https://shift.store/sg1fan23477/retail

www.ingramcontent.com/pod-product-compliance
Lightning Source LLC
Chambersburg PA
CBHW012145140726
47991CB00009B/3171